FIRST PRAYERS

Bellwood Press, 1233 Central St., Evanston, IL 60201-0605

Printed in Mexico on acid-free paper ∞

14 13 12 11 4 3 2 1

Library of Congress Cataloging-in-Publication Data

'Abdu'l-Bahá, 1844–1921.
First prayers : for tender plants : prayers / by 'Abdu'l-Baha.
p. cm.
Includes bibliographical references and index.
ISBN 978-0-87743-715-4 (alk. paper)
1. Bahai children—Prayers and devotions. I. Title.
BP363.A3 2011c
297.9'3433—dc23
2011040485

Artwork by Charity Hofert
Book design by C. Aaron Kreader

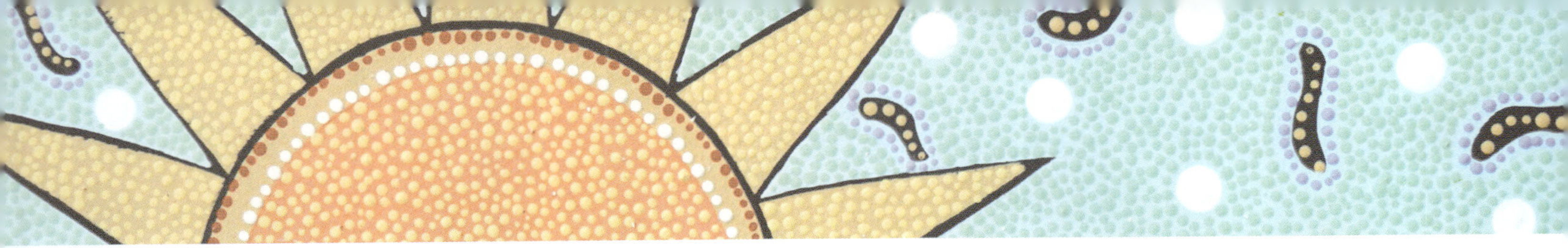

FIRST PRAYERS

For Tender Plants

Prayers by 'Abdu'l-Bahá

BELLWOOD PRESS
Evanston, Illinois

1 He is God!

He is God!

O God, my God!

Bestow upon me
a pure heart,

like unto a pearl.

—'Abdu'l-Bahá

2 O God,

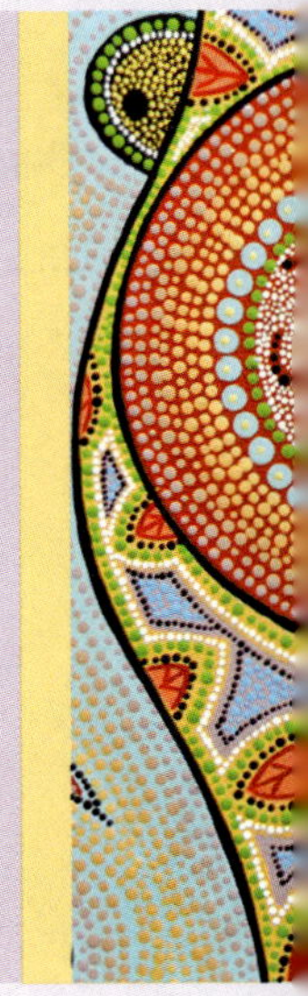

O God,

guide me,
protect me,

make of me
a shining lamp

and a
brilliant star.

Thou art the Mighty

and the Powerful.

—'Abdu'l-Bahá

3 O Lord!

O Lord!

I am a child;

enable me to grow

beneath the shadow
of Thy loving-kindness.

I am a tender plant;
cause me to be nurtured

through the outpourings
of the clouds of Thy bounty.

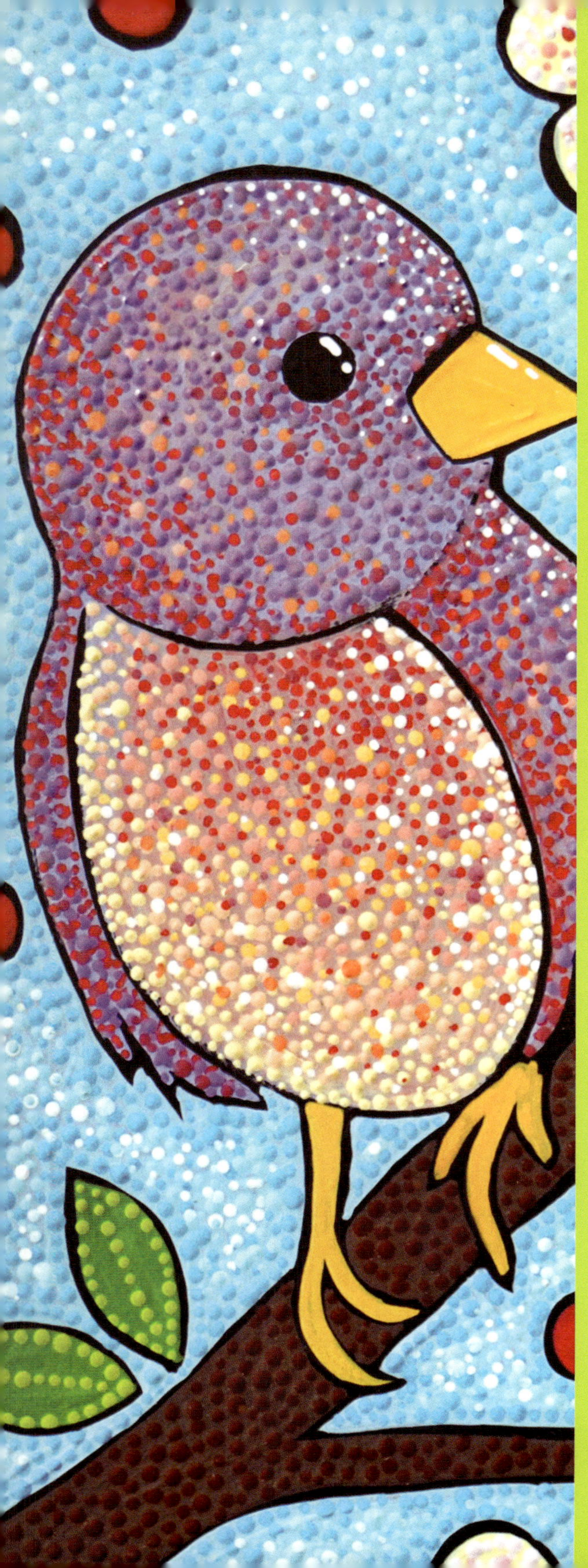

I am a sapling of the garden of love;

make me into a
fruitful tree.

Thou art the Mighty
and the Powerful,

and Thou art
the All-Loving,

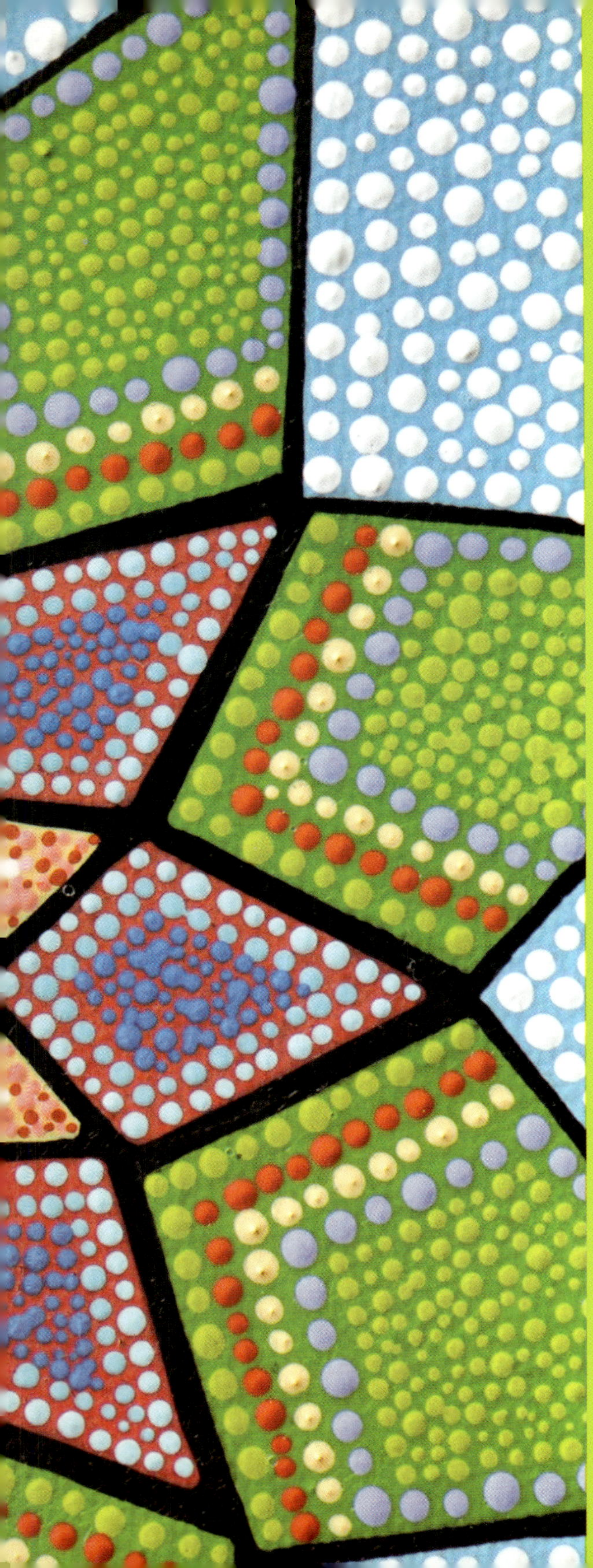

the All-Knowing,

the All-Seeing.

—'Abdu'l-Bahá

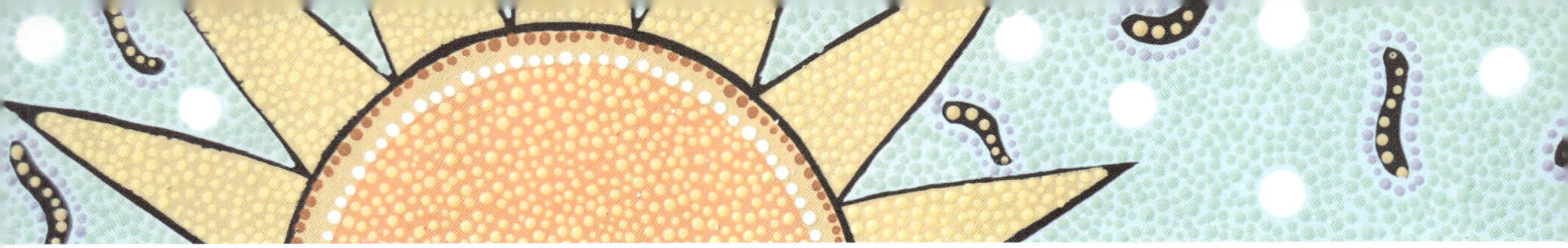

BELLWOOD PRESS
Evanston, Illinois